Dictate
YOUR BOOK

HOW TO WRITE YOUR BOOK
FASTER, BETTER, AND SMARTER

MONICA LEONELLE

Contents

GET ON THE ARC LIST!

If you're interested in getting Advanced Reading Copies (ARCs) of upcoming books in the Growth Hacking For Storytellers series, please go here for instructions:

ProseOnFire.com/Reviewers

As an independent author, reviews are one of the most important ways I have to get the word out. Your review will encourage others to grab the book. Go to ProseOnFire. com/pofd if you want to leave a review of Dictate Your Book and help others discover a new way to write!

INTRODUCTION

Hello there, and thank you for picking up this book! My name is Monica Leonelle and I've been an avid user and advocate of dictation software since 2012. I have used it to dictate the first drafts of at least 20 different books, including this one you're reading right here!

For those of you who don't know my story, let me give you the CliffNotes version:

2009 - I published my first book. Yay!

2010 - I didn't publish a book. This business was tougher than I thought.

2011 - My first fiction book came out! I was thrilled.

2012 - I published two more shorter fiction books, both mid-sized novellas. Still not a ton of momentum. But one of those books, I wrote in two days using productivity techniques I had learned as a freelancer. I posted it under a pen name, and it is still on the market today!

2013 - I published another book, a rewrite of an early one from 2011. Still not a ton of momentum. But I knew that I was onto something with increasing my writing productivity—it just hadn't quite "clicked" yet. That's when I experimented heavily with dictation and embarked on a 2-month long writing experiment to improve my writing speed and consistency. I ended that experiment in November 2013, and that's when things got interesting in my author career.

2014 - I knew how to write fast after all that experimentation. Now it was time to work. And work I did, putting out eight books and one short story with the help of one amazing collaborator. This was also the first year I made a consistent $1000 a month several months in a row just from my books—something I'd been trying to do for five years previously.

2015 - Remember that 2-month experiment I did in 2013? That experiment became the basis for a book I published in early 2015, called *Write Better, Faster: How To Triple Your Writing Speed and Write More Every Day*. Because I talked about dictation throughout the book, I started getting a lot of questions about dictation from other authors. I wrote Dictate Your Book to answer those questions and share my own experiences with and philosophies toward dictation, all in one easy reference guide.

Also in 2015 - I'm on track to publish at least 17 books this year across three different imprints. If all goes well, I should have 22 books published in this year alone! So obviously dictation is working for me—and I think it can work for you too.

If you are interested in a fuller story about my background in writing productivity and want to know how I reached writing speeds of 4000+ words per hour, Write Better, Faster has everything you wanted to know and more.

And if you are just starting out and want to build a daily writing habit, you'll love the strategies I share in The 8-Minute Writing Habit, which is aimed at busy people who need a writing routine that integrates with their lifestyle. All three books are available as part of the Growth Hacking For Storytellers series, which helps authors improve their productivity, nail their craft, and sell more books.

In *Dictate Your Book,* I share:

- Why dictation is one of the most important skills you can learn as an author
- How dictation protects your long-term author career and keeps you healthy
- Why dictation is for everyone—not just extroverts, or public speakers, or tech whizzes
- How to figure out if dictation will work for you with free apps and software that you can access on any device
- How to get over the initial hurdles of using dictation in your regular workflow
- My complete equipment list of everything I use for my home setup, my Walk 'n' Talks, and more
- How I prep my work for dictation so that I can have the most productive sessions possible
- How I've achieved ~98% accuracy in any room, on any device
- How I learn dictation commands for punctuation and formatting quickly and efficiently without feeling overwhelmed
- Why I don't bother with dictation drills
- All my best dictation shortcuts and workarounds for any frustrations that come up with the software

This book contains 50-60 of my best tips on dictation, coming from my personal experience of having used it to massively up my writing game for the past three years. I know in my heart that even if you've tried dictation before and hated it, or even if this is your first introduction to it, the strategies in this book will give you a lot to think about and implement. Dictation has changed my life and career and it might change yours too—in fact, I hope it does.

Chapter 1
WHY YOU SHOULD DICTATE

Why should you dictate? It's a question that's probably been on your mind for a while, especially if you've been writing for several years. After all, you already have a multitude of ways of getting your words out. You can handwrite them in a notebook or journal, you can use a typewriter, or you can do what most of us do—use a keyboard and a word processor to draft our books.

So why add yet another piece of technology that enables us to do the same exact thing that we're already doing? It's a fair question, so I'm going to spend this chapter giving you a multitude of reasons why now is the time to get on board with this fascinating way of writing that is giving tons of successful authors an edge over their competition.

REASON #1: BECAUSE YOU CAN!

The technology is here, why not use it?

The first reason that you should learn dictation is a pretty simple one—because you can learn dictation. This is not technology that won't be ready for public consumption until the far-flung future. We have the technology to do dictation right now, and this is an unprecedented way of writing that we've never been able to do before—even as early as ten years ago.

I believe when you're given technology to do your job better, it makes sense to take advantage of it. It's an opportunity that millions of writers and storytellers who lived before us did not have. Give it a try for no other reason than that you were born in a certain time period and have lived to see this incredible day.

REASON #2: BECAUSE IT'S THE FUTURE

Consider your ancestors. Imagine someone telling you that they still do all their work on the typewriter just because they can't quite get the hang of a PC. You might be one of these people already, or you might be someone rolling your eyes at those people.

Now, imagine the typewriter just came out and you have an author friend who says they would prefer to write out their novels by hand, thank you very much! Still not rolling your eyes?

In the near future—like the next ten years—other authors may be rolling their eyes at you because you never hopped on board the dictation train. Dictation is here to stay and it's going to become more and more commonplace not just for authors, but for everybody. We're already seeing children who are learning to interact with smartphones using their voices rather than typing on a keyboard. We're already seeing our Xboxes and our televisions being activated by voice command rather than with a remote control. We're already seeing YouTube videos and podcasting overtaking blogging and other simpler media forms in popularity.

The world is changing faster than we can keep up with. The concepts that were in science fiction movies 15 years ago are now a reality. Voice instruction, dictation, and recognition are available now. It's only going to get more prevalent. You can start now for what is inevitable—hands-free control of every object and tool we know of in the world.

I encourage you to embrace this technology while you still have an opportunity to learn it at your own pace. You don't want to be caught trying to learn something after everyone is already using it to lap you in book production and sales. If you're serious about becoming an author, dictation is one of those must-have skills that is going to increase the longevity of your career.

REASON #3: BECAUSE IT'S FASTER

Dictation is more popular than ever in 2015 among authors, especially as the technology has gotten better and better and several new books about writing faster have come out. One of them that kicked off the year in March was my own, entitled Write Better, Faster. In it, I talk about how dictation took me from 2000 words per hour to over 4000 words per hour in certain sessions. After this book came out, hundreds of authors came forward with their own experiences with dictation. Many agreed that dictation helps double or sometimes even triple their word counts and has helped them produce content significantly faster than they were able to do before.

In the book *5000 Words Per Hour,* Chris Fox gives his full system for how he uses dictation to get to over 5000 words per hour. In *The Writer's Guide to Training Your Dragon: Using Speech Recognition Software to Dictate Your Book and Supercharge Your Writing Workflow,* Scott Baker shares how writers can tame their Dragons and improve their accuracy while dicating All of these books are following a trend, that dictation and other voice-activated controllers are becoming more and more prevalent in our world. As authors, we need to sit up and pay attention to the incredible productivity gains we can get from learning dictation.

If you are interested in writing two or three times as fast as you currently are, there's no better way to do this than to start using dictation. Dictation will help you write better and write faster. It's a much smarter way to get your first draft on, and imagine what you could accomplish if you are producing twice as many books every single year for the rest of your life. The gains are simply too huge to ignore, and you can bet that other authors in your genre are not ignoring them!

REASON #4: BECAUSE IT ADDS REDUNDANCY

Do you intend to be a writer for the rest of your life?

For most of us, I imagine the answer to this question is yes. The problem is that many of us are reliant on our ability to continue doing the work into our golden years. For some of us, our golden years may be upon us or getting closer and closer. For others, we're just getting started in life, though it's never too early to pay attention to future health concerns.

When I was learning dictation, one of my motivators was to add redundancy to my writing ability. What do I mean by that? At the time, the only way that I could work was by putting my hands and fingers to keyboard or by scribbling notes in my journal. Both of these required my hands to be in great working order.

What I found, however, was that my writing habit was taking a huge toll on the health of my hands. I was developing soreness, wrist problems, and I was also forced to stare at the screen most of the time while typing.

When I started learning dictation, many of those problems went away. I was able to instead use my voice to get words onto the screen, which means that even if my hands are not able to type in the future, or not able to type as quickly, I'll still have a way to get my writing done.

If you have similar health concerns or feel pain in your hands and wrists after a long typing session, this may be a huge motivation to dictate for either some or all of your writing sessions.

Note, of course, that I'm not saying that your voice could not have health issues as well, but in that case you know that you can type instead of speak. I'm also not saying stop typing, and in fact I think typing is going to be an extremely useful skill set in the future when fewer people are able to do it. All I'm saying is that having two ways to input words is much better than having only one, especially when it comes to your long-term health, which we don't always have full control over.

REASON #5: BECAUSE IT'S ERGONOMIC

Dictation can also help you with your office ergonomics in many ways. For starters, it does give your hands a break, which is fantastic especially when you're trying to create content quickly. For myself, when I started writing over 2000 words per hour for hours in a row, my hands were in so much pain. Many other authors have shared similar challenges with me as they increased their speeds—but luckily, dictation helps avoid this!

In addition to protecting your hands and wrists, dictation frees you from the typical office position that is killing so many of us. We all know the dangers of sitting at a desk for 8 to 10 hours a day, but most of us have no way of avoiding this. It's impossible because we work in front of our screens, and for many of us, we don't have a ton of meetings or movement that can break up our routine. Dictation frees us from this constraint because we don't need to be in front of a computer while we dictate. You could do what I'm doing at this exact moment, which is pacing around my living room as I speak my book out loud into a microphone that's connected directly to my computer.

You could also do a setup that I love implementing during the fall and springtime when it's not too hot outside. I'll take my work with me on a long walk outside and dictate my content into a recorder, which I then bring back to my computer and get transcribed using Dragon Dictate. I call these my Walk 'n' Talks, and I'll be sharing with you later in this book exactly how to get set up with the technology that you need to do them.

To be clear, it's not healthy to speak into a microphone for 8 to 10 hours a day while walking any more than it is to be sitting at a desk. The goal of ergonomics is to constantly be changing your environment so that you're not in the same position over and over again. Dictation gives you the opportunity to spend a couple hours a day walking around your office, not tied to a screen, or taking a break outside and getting a little bit of exercise while enjoying nature. I can assure you you'll still have plenty of computer time, because unfortunately not everything can be dictated—at least not yet!

REASON #6: BECAUSE YOU CAN MULTITASK

I've already talked about how dictation can help you ergonomically and even let you get some exercise during the day if you take your setup on the road. But don't let my personal uses limit you. If you get a Bluetooth headset microphone, you could be writing or dictating while you do almost anything. You could do it while you're in the car, washing the dishes, or at your boring job filing a bunch of paperwork. As long as the other task is somewhat mindless, you could be dictating during that time.

Many people have trouble finding time during their day to write their draft because they have a full-time job or a family to take care of. With a little bit of preparation and imagination, you could spend those mindless minutes doing something that helps further your author career. You could write your entire first draft in the wasted moments of your busy day!

Here are some additional opportunities to multitask with dictation:

- While doing simple exercises, like squats, lunges, or weights
- While doing any chore around the house
- While waiting on the kids to get ready for something
- While cooking dinner for the family
- While walking the dog

7

- While getting dressed or completing other mindless morning routine tasks (brushing your teeth excluded)

Any task that doesn't take up much of your mind space is a prime opportunity for getting some dictation in.

REASON #7: BECAUSE IT REMOVES INTERNET DISTRACTIONS

You won't be able to dictate and use the internet at once. And since the internet is one of our largest distractions, you can actually get much more done because dictation is going to force you away from the Internet.

When you're writing, it's easy to shift back and forth between your manuscript and the internet. You tell yourself that you're doing research or you're taking a quick break while you think about the next part of your book. Then, an hour goes by and all your lives are gone on Candy Crush, and now it's bedtime and you haven't written any more words. Sound familiar?

Dictation completely circumvents this procrastination technique and forces you to do your writing.

One last thing for those of you who have families. If you've made a deal with your spouse that they watch the kids for thirty minutes while you get more of your draft done, dictation is going to give you that extra bit of accountability. Because your entire family is going to know whether you did it or not—they're going to be able to hear you! As you dictate, it's natural that people who live with you are going to notice. You'll be aware that they are aware, which is going to make you much more accountable to your writing habit.

REASON #8: BECAUSE YOU CAN'T EDIT WHILE WRITING

In addition to the internet, there is one other thing that dictation is going to keep you from doing, and that's editing.

One of the reasons that most writers get so few words done on their draft per hour or per day is because they can't separate the writing and the editing processes. Dictation is going to force you to separate those two tasks because it's so difficult to edit your book out loud. Instead, you're going to get into the flow of speaking, which means you're in the flow of writing automatically. You don't even have to think about it or force yourself back to focus, because you really can't focus on anything else besides what's in your mind. There are no other stimuli to distract you.

REASON #9: BECAUSE TELLING STORIES OUT LOUD IS IN OUR HISTORY

If none of these major benefits have convinced you to try dictation yet, I have one more that might tug at your emotions.

As you decide to type away your next draft, just remember that the keyboard is a recent, man-made invention. Humans do not naturally tell stories using words via written text. Historically, we've shared stories using images with narrative via the spoken word.

So if you're worried that you won't be able to tell a story out loud, just keep in mind that it's in your DNA. Even if it feels uncomfortable at first, you're going to get used to it very quickly. It's ingrained in humans to tell stories out loud around campfires. Never forget that, because it's going to help you through any challenges you may have while embracing this new technology.

Chapter 2
WILL DICTATION WORK FOR YOU?

Ever since my first book in the Growth Hacking For Storytellers series Write Better, Faster came out, I have received dozens of questions about dictation. The number one question that writers have is whether dictation will work for them. I even get feedback from authors who have tried dictation and decided that it will not, in fact, work for them.

So will it work for you?

My answer is a resounding "Yes!"—but only if you want it to.

I believe that dictation can work for anybody, it just depends on that particular writer's dedication to learning a new skill set.

Let me reframe the question. Imagine you're talking to a new author who is just getting started with writing. Imagine that they come up to you and ask, "Will writing on a computer work for me?"

You'd probably be wondering to yourself, "Why is this a concern to her?" It seems quite silly to imagine that writing on a computer, which is how almost every writer completes his or her book, would be a question mark in anybody's mind.

Well, the same is true with dictation. Keep in mind that dictation is simply another technology for getting words out into the world. Dictation can work for you if you are willing to learn a new set of skills, the same way a washing machine can work for you if you are willing to do your laundry in a different way.

So, in my opinion, it's ultimately up to you whether dictation is going to work for you. There are some people who say that dictation is only for authors with no accent, is only for extroverts, is only for authors with public speaking experience, and so on. I may have even said some of these myself in the past. (I was wrong!)

Now you know the truth—dictation is for everyone. It's an extremely affordable technology that has made huge gains in the last ten years. It uses your voice commands to input your words to a computer with a 95% accuracy rate. Just like all other technology that came before it, including telephones, computers, dishwashers, toasters, and more, the technology is available to anyone in a first world country who is interested in taking advantage of it.

In this chapter, I'll give you tons of information about how you can make dictation happen for you. I believe that once you buy in to the mindset I've used to approach dictation, you'll have a much easier time getting it to work for you.

TEST DICTATION FOR FREE FIRST

The best way to learn whether dictation is going to work for you is to just try it! However, before you go out and get a bunch of equipment to do dictation long-term, you can actually test the concept for free—which I highly recommend as a first step.

There are several ways you can do this:

- **Voice Command Software** - Most smartphones have some version of voice command built in. You may be familiar with Siri or the "Ok Google" prompt. If you don't own a smartphone, check your car system, your Xbox, or your television. The next time you're using one of these devices, instead of texting or reaching for the remote, give voice command a shot and see if you can get the technology to respond the way you want.

- **Dictation Apps** - To test dictation specifically, you can download an app on your phone, tablet, or computer. The one I recommend which is available on phones and tablets is Dragon Dictation, which has a free version. (There are dozens of other dictation apps you could try as well, however Nuance is the market leader in the space at the time of this writing.) With this app, you can speak for about four or five continuous minutes into your phone, and then you can email yourself the results.

- **Notetaking Apps** - Most apps like Evernote have a voice command option, so you could dictate directly into the Evernote app and it will capture your content. This works on both the mobile app and the desktop app. Many authors are already familiar with Evernote and may even have the Premium account, so this is a great way to get started without downloading any new software.

- **Speech-to-Text on Your Computer** - Many computers have some sort of dictation software built-in. My experience with these is that they aren't quite good enough to use on a daily basis, but they are good enough to get your feet wet and get comfortable with the idea of dictation. If you do short writing sessions (as I suggest in The 8-Minute Writing Habit) you may be able to get by with this technology alone.

- **Browser Apps** - If you want to try this out but don't have the right software, you can test dictation right over the internet. The two browser apps I know of are TalkTyper (http://talktyper.com) and Speechpad (http://Speechpad.pw).

Word of warning for all of these options: none of them are particularly suitable for long-term ongoing or daily use. I share them not to recommend them as your dictation solution, but rather to give you options for testing dictation without purchasing any software or equipment. Many of these options have poorer accuracy than the professional software, or they have great accuracy but length or time limitations. (TalkTyper, for example, limits you to a single sentence or thought before you have to start the dictation again.)

Use these options to test dictation, but if you decide to go for it, make sure you upgrade to the regular software. My recommendation is Dragon Natural Speaking for Windows or Dragon Dictate for Mac. Both are from the same company, Nuance.

You can purchase and download them immediately here:

ProseOnFire.com/Dragon/

EASE INTO DICTATION SLOWLY

One of the biggest mistakes I see authors make when attempting dictation is trying to incorporate it into their regular workflow immediately. They pull up whatever novel or non-fiction chapter they are working on right then and try to dictate it instead of using their keyboard.

Huge mistake! This, to me, is the top reason that many authors give up on dictation too early.

Before you try to drastically change your workflow, I highly recommend easing into dictation slowly. Here's my simple training plan:

First, set your novel aside and don't even touch your regular writing routine at this point. Too many authors think, "I'm already good at writing, this is just another input method." Just because you're a great writer doesn't mean you'll be great at dictation. World-champion tennis player Serena Williams wouldn't walk onto a professional basketball game and say, "I'm already good at sports, this is just a different ball and different play rules than I'm used to."

Next, build dictation into your daily life and learn with a project where the stakes for success are much smaller. You can dictate email drafts, blog posts, or texts using dictation, for example.

Finally, once you are able to dictate a text, a business email, and a blog post with minimal errors, you can start dictating for a portion of your normal writing session— maybe 15 minutes to start.

If you use this simple training plan, when you are ready to switch over for the bulk of your writing sessions, you'll have already built the basic skill set you need and won't be distracted by the technology. You can focus on the writing, just as you do now while typing on your keyboard!

WORK THROUGH FRUSTRATIONS

You are going to get frustrated—it's natural!

Consider how a master pianist feels when she picks up a guitar for the first time. She has a lot of the knowledge needed to play that guitar, but there's still a lot to learn. She may be able to read music, and she may understand the concept of chords. However, she's going to need to learn where fingers should be positioned and how to use the pick. She'll also need to get comfortable holding the guitar and learn how to tune and maintain it.

Still, if she works through those beginning pains and initial frustrations, she will probably be fluent in guitar sooner than a student who's been playing for years already!

As a serious writer, you are in the very best position among all other people in the world to do well with dictation, because you have already built so many of the skill sets needed for it. You will probably pick up dictation skills quickly. Just keep in mind that there will be some parts of it that you need to work at before you're entirely comfortable.

And if you feel frustrated at any point in your training, remember that at some point in your life you had to learn to type. There's nothing about typing that comes naturally or intuitively, and you probably had to rewire your brain a bit to memorize the odd positioning of the keys and how to type without looking down at your fingers.

Learning to type probably wasn't that easy, but eventually you learned.

Similarly, you are rewiring your brain for a new dictation skill set. It will take a bit of time. Work through those frustrations rather than giving up!

HANG ON TO YOUR KEYBOARD!

This is the funniest thing. When authors first start thinking about switching to dictation, they feel like they are losing their keyboard.

The truth is that there's no real "switching" involved. Don't worry about having to give up or trade in something that's already working for you. Instead, think of it more like adding capacity. You're just adding another opportunity and skill set to produce more words!

As you're learning dictation, don't put pressure on yourself to use it at all times. I don't dictate all the time—not even close. I still spend many of my writing hours in front of the computer doing outlining, editing, or even drafting. I also write on my smartphone and I use my iPad and connecting keyboard to write in bed.

So continue to utilize your other workflows, and you'll find dictation simpler and more fun to learn because there will be no pressure to make it work until you're ready.

Chapter 3

GET STARTED WITH DICTATION QUICKLY

So you've now tried dictation and you can see yourself using this option on a regular basis. Great! Once you've decided that yes, you are going to commit to dictation, you'll probably need to do a little bit of work to get yourself set up.

Unfortunately, the tools that you used to test the concept of dictation are not going to be the same tools you want to use every single day in your regular workflow. These tools are simply too inconvenient, and if you're taking this writing thing seriously, you probably want to do dictation properly. This chapter is going to help you get set up with dictation and integrate it into your current workflow so that you can transition between typing and dictation fluidly. Remember, our goal for dictation is simply to add more capacity. We're not trying to trade anything in or out. That means that your workflow still needs to incorporate opportunity for typing so that when typing makes more sense for your project, you can switch back and forth seamlessly.

DECIDE ON YOUR WORKFLOW

FIGURE OUT THE TECH

Dictation requires three tech pieces:
- A way to tell your computer what to put on the screen, usually through a microphone
- A connection between your dictation software and your voice commands, either happening in real-time with a line-in or by recording your voice and sending the audio file to your software
- A way for your dictation software to translate your voice commands into text on your screen, usually in real-time, but possibly after the fact using the transcription option

If you choose not to get the dictation software, you'll need to replace it with an actual person transcribing your audio files to text. I don't recommend this option because it is quite expensive in comparison to using dictation software.

Another aspect you want to consider is whether you prefer to be mobile or if you're okay being tethered to your computer with a long cord. I personally have two setups, one for standing or sitting near my computer (connected to it with a line-in) and one for on-the-go that's a little more complicated. I'll talk about equipment in the next section so you can see what it will take.

CHOOSE YOUR WRITING PHASES

After you've figured out the technical side of your workflow, you'll also want to decide where dictation fits in. Are you going to use it at the draft stage, the outlining stage, or somewhere in-between?

I recommend using dictation for pre-production (outline, beats, sketches, etc.) and the first draft only.

You can edit your content with dictation but it's quite a bit more complicated than drafting. You'll need to dig in to your dictation software and learn commands to move the cursor around, select and delete text, change the formatting of specific words, and more. This is going to overwhelm you if you try to do it when you're just starting out. I'll share more tips about learning commands in a later chapter, but for now, assume that editing your book using dictation is an advanced topic.

ADD A CLEANUP PHASE

Next, you'll want an easy system for cleanup on your manuscript to fix any errors you or the software makes. I personally do most of this in post-production, for the reasons I stated about the difficulty of editing above. However, you do want to get a feel for the software and make a decision, since it will affect your workflow and potentially add an extra step.

The easiest way to do this and the way I personally use is to do cleanup at the same time you do edits. I'll talk more specifically about how I do this later, but the gist is that I do a quick proof and rely heavily on the Replace All function right before I do any actual revision (content or line-editing, etc.). I tend to do this by scene rather than on the whole document at once.

You can also hire an assistant to reproof your draft before you edit if that works better for you. This is good for minor dictation errors, but bad if your Dragon is producing gobbledygook for you.

CREATE YOUR TRAINING PLAN

Finally, you want a process for "training your Dragon" so that accuracy improves over time. This doesn't need to be complicated. I've trained my Dragon primarily by using it, but there are some tips and tricks that might be worth doing if your accuracy is not where you want it to be in an upcoming chapter.

You certainly don't have to do it the way I do it, and you also don't have to make all these decisions right now. I provided this section because we are about to talk about what equipment to get, and it helps to have an idea of how you intend to use dictation before you go out and purchase the technology.

GET THE EQUIPMENT

At the bare minimum you'll need:

#1 - DICTATION SOFTWARE

My recommendation (hands down) is Dragon Natural Speaking (Windows) or Dragon Dictate (Mac) by Nuance, the current market leader in dictation software. This software is fairly affordable and has come a long way in the last 3-4 years since I have been using it. They boast rates of 99% accuracy, so it's likely to work for you.

You can purchase and download it immediately here:

ProseOnFire.com/Dragon/

There may be other great software on the market worth trying, but I'll admit that I haven't tried it and can't speak to its value.

This book assumes you are using Dragon, and I've customized the tips and tricks to fit Dragon's commands.

#2 - A GOOD MICROPHONE

Dragon software typically comes with a microphone, or you can use the one built in to your computer; however, I recommend getting a microphone that's at least podcast quality. You will get much better audio with the latter, which means Dragon can translate your speech to text with more accuracy. I have personally found that simply having a better microphone makes a world of difference in my accuracy rate.

The microphone I have is the AT2020 by Audio Technica; however, I believe any mic that's popular for podcasting will work. The other one I see recommended frequently is the Blue Yeti mic. Both are around the same price, so it just depends on what you prefer and what other features you're looking for.

I don't want to get into a huge discussion about condenser vs. dynamic mics at this time. What I will say about it is that most radio stations use dynamic mics for recording. Both the AT2020 and the Blue Yeti are condenser mics, so if you want a great sound, you can upgrade to a dynamic mic that gets tons of recommendations for podcasting called the RODE Podcaster. This is priced a little higher than the other two, but it's the third option I'd go with if you need a microphone recommendation.

You can get these microphones below:

AT2020:

proseonfire.com/at2020/

Blue Yeti:

proseonfire.com/yeti/

RODE Podcaster:

proseonfire.com/rode/

These will usually come with an XLR cord or a USB connection, but make sure you read the descriptions carefully to ensure that you are getting all the cords and connections you need to hook this up to your computer.

#3 - A CONNECTION TO PLUG IN

I highly recommend buying the XLR version of whatever mic you use. Some condenser mics connect with a USB cord, but this will limit your usability if you decide to take your setup on the go or use your mic for a different purpose. I also prefer to be able to change out the cables when needed, as the wiring between a mic and a computer can get damaged easily if you're taking your setup on the go.

If you have an XLR connector for you mic you will need something to convert it to USB so you can plug in to your computer. I use the Icicle Mic Converter by Blue Microphones (which I often just call my "blue icicle" in interviews). This will supply the 48V phantom power needed for your condenser mic.

Just to set your expectations, when you receive your blue icicle it's going to look and feel like the cheapest piece of plastic you've ever spent $40 on. But it works great! I've had mine for three or four years and it's still kicking! Get it below:

ProseOnFire.com/Icicle/

OPTIONAL EQUIPMENT

The first three items I mentioned are the least you'll need to use dictation in your daily workflow, in my opinion. I've also put together a list of accessories that I believe are worth the investment:

#4 - A MIC STAND AND POP FILTER

I currently have an adjustable desk stand to hold my mic and use a 6-inch circular pop filter in front of it. You can also get a boom stand, which sits on the floor. The latter gives you a ton more mobility for positioning your mic, which is great if you are doing podcast interviews or videos to market your book.

You can get these specific accessories below:

Mic Desk Stand:

proseonfire.com/micstand/

Pop Filter:

proseonfire.com/popfilter/

Boom Stand (no specific recommendation):

proseonfire.com/boomstand/

#5 - EXTRA CABLES

Because I rely so heavily on my dictation setup for both dictation and other media needs (podcasts, screencasts, videos) I have double of much of my equipment, including my blue icicle, the XLR cords (which come in multiple lengths, good for extending your pacing distance from the computer), and my iRig PRE (which I'll get to in a minute). I didn't buy these right away, but have collected them over the years.

ON-THE-GO EQUIPMENT

If you intend to take your setup on the go, you'll need just a few more items to make it work:

#6 - YOUR MOBILE DEVICE + A RECORDER APP

If you have a smartphone or a tablet that runs on iOS or Android, you should be able to download a recording app to capture your voice while you are away from your computer. You will not be able to get speech-to-text in real-time, so you will instead need to record an audio file of you speaking and run it through your dictation software later.

I tested several recorder apps and settled on HD Recorder Plus. I recommend trying a few apps yourself before purchasing to see what you like. Most apps have a free trial version and a paid upgrade.

#7 - A CONNECTION TO PLUG IN ON THE GO

Just like you needed a connector to get your mic to your computer, you also need a connector to get your mic to your device. I use the iRig PRE by IK Multimedia, but there are plenty of other options you could try. The iRig PRE is again a pretty cheap piece of plastic. I found it to be a bit touchy on the go and ended up having to tape over the volume dial so that it didn't move while I was walking (imagine you're speaking for 20 minutes with your volume all the way down—yep, it happened to me and that recording was unusable).

Whichever connector you get, make sure you also purchase two sets of batteries and a recharger. I go through about 2/3rds of a battery every time I go on a walk.

ProseOnFire.com/irig

#8 - A WIND SCREEN

This serves the same purpose as the pop filter in your home setup. It is used to protect your mic from your spit. It also helps block out outdoor sounds so they don't contaminate your recording. If you don't want to buy one of these, you can use a (clean) sock. I still haven't purchased a wind screen for some reason—I guess the sock works just fine for me at the moment. But you will get looks from passerbys, so maybe a wind screen isn't a bad investment.

ProseOnFire.com/windscreen

#9 - A DEDICATED RECORDER

This may be the simpler option for you, depending on your setup. Nuance sells a few dedicated recorders for Windows users that works with Dragon Natural Speaking. I haven't tested it because I'm on Mac, but there are some interesting syncing features and uses that may be valuable to you if you are conducting in-person interviews that you want to transcribe for your book notes or draft. It's also sometimes just easier to have an all-in-one solution!

ProseOnFire.com/dictationrecorder/

As you look at this list of equipment, try not to feel overwhelmed. Remember, you can get started with just the first three items on the list. I did not order all my equipment right away, but rather collected it over the course of several months. I strongly recommend viewing dictation as a long-term project that you are putting together a little at a time. It's not going to happen overnight, but as you get familiar with the technology, you'll see that it's really not that complicated to get set up and incorporate dictation into your daily workflow.

PREP YOUR WORK

Once you've gotten all the equipment you need, you're ready to get started with a project.

But it probably won't be quite that straightforward.

In order to start dictating or recording your project, you first need to make sure your work is prepped in a way that makes sense with dictation.

What works best for me is to have a set of beats for each scene synced up with all my devices using an app called Evernote.

For those of you not familiar with beats, they are an expansion of your outline, about one paragraph of notes per every 300-500 words of your draft.

You can learn more about the way I do beats by grabbing my 4-step process for beating writer's block at:

http://proseonfire.com/tracking/

If I'm doing a Walk 'n' Talk, I bring two different devices—one for recording and one for looking at my beats. (Note: these are two devices I already own, an iPad and my smartphone.) You can also compile your beats and put them on your Kindle if that's easier, or if you don't have a second device, you could print them out or write them up in a notebook by hand.

You could also just work from an outline, but I've found that for me I am able to speak my scene more easily when I have put in the extra work to do the beats. It's difficult to get into flow with just the outline, but your mileage may vary. And if you want to save time, you can also dictate your beats first, which I do quite often!

TEST AND ITERATE

As you get more comfortable with your equipment and workflow, remember that you can always change anything that's not working. I've shared what works for me, but you should test your setup, your workflow, and your equipment to find what works best for you. I believe that the best way to make progress is to get a system—any system—in place, then iterate until it's finely tuned to your needs and liking. Stay positive toward this fun experiment you've embarked on and enjoy the process of learning something new!

Chapter 4
DICTATION TIPS AND TRICKS

In this chapter, i'll share my tips and tricks for what works and what doesn't, based on my personal experiences with dictation and Dragon. I've divided it into four sections based on the questions I get asked most: accuracy, movement, commands, and frustrations.

PART A: ACCURACY

The frustration I see most for authors is how to improve Dragon's accuracy.

Here are a few tips that have helped me immensely:

CREATE A CUSTOM USER PROFILE

You can create multiple custom user profiles upon launching Dragon, which I highly recommend. If you are sharing Dragon with someone else in your family, you definitely want different profiles for each user. Each user is going to train their Dragon drastically differently due to each voice having a unique sound and intonation when speaking certain words and phrases.

I also have profiles for each different microphone I've used (I have since narrowed that down to only my AT2020, but I originally tested a variety of mic inputs).

You may also want a custom profile for different rooms or houses you work from, at least to start. Noise and acoustics change from room to room, so this is important early on when you're training your Dragon. For some people, this may be overkill, but I enjoy testing so I wanted to be able to control for this variable as well.

While most of my custom profiles work pretty well, I have one profile that produces extremely accurate output and is generally a cut above the rest. I now use this one almost exclusively. The way it got to that point was through testing various setups until I found the best setup for training. Now, I use that profile in any location and it works fantastically. And because I use it all the time, I have years of history with it, so the accuracy has gotten even better over the years.

When you are testing, you want to create many profiles, but once you find the one you love try to stick with it. I've noticed that a Dragon profile gets better with age, just like wine.

That said, don't commit to a Dragon profile too soon. You'll be investing lots of time and energy into your best profile, so make sure you date for a while.

I know this advice will probably beg the question, "But when is too soon?" The only way I can answer is, "When she's the one, you'll just know."

DO THE TRAINING

Dragon comes with several training exercises that you can do when you first create a custom user profile. You typically only have to complete one of the trainings to move forward with the software, but I recommend doing all of them. This trains your Dragon quickly and gives you feedback as you are going by highlighting words and phrases that the software didn't pick up.

As you are doing the training, make sure to speak as naturally as possible so you are training it to understand the normal way you would talk. I sometimes purposely speak "sloppily" into the mic, not bothering to over-enunciate or even sit that closely to my microphone. This more accurately mimics how I dictate day-to-day, because there will be plenty of days when I feel lazy or just don't want to work that hard to get my words in.

EAT THE MIC

When I was in an acoustic jazz choir in high school, everyone had their own mic and the director would frequently yell, "Eat the mic!"

What she meant by that was put your mouth right up next to your mic so it captures your clearest voice with less ambient noise. This is most important for accuracy. If you are struggling with dictation accuracy, eating the mic will improve your situation greatly.

To best eat the mic, I recommend either a pop filter or wind screen (both discussed in the last chapter) to protect your mic from spit, which will naturally happen when you get that close. You are basically kissing the microphone while your parents are watching out the window with the porch light on (no tongue).

I also recommend a boom stand, as the desk stand will force you to lean forward or lean over your desk and might be less comfortable.

Not everyone will need to eat the mic all the time. I am able to sit back in my chair now and speak, and Dragon still translates my words accurately. Test this for yourself and you'll soon find your most comfortable distance from the mic. But if accuracy is a problem, eat that mic!

SPEAK WITH CONFIDENCE

Dragon loves confidence. It works best when you follow this process:

- Think the sentence
- Speak the sentence (adding proper punctuation)

If you struggle with speaking with confidence, try standing up and walking around the room as you dictate (this requires a longer XLR cord). I often pretend I have an audience and I'm trying to entertain them as I speak. For introverts, it may help to pretend you're putting on a dictation performance.

PART B: MOVEMENT

Ever since I first started talking about Walk 'n' Talks, I've had tons of questions about how to take dictation on the go. If you are a fan of the idea of standing desks, you'll probably love these tips:

STAND UP, WALK AROUND

I'm a strong believer that you have to get moving physically if you want to get moving mentally. If you are slogging through your dictation, try standing up. It's good for most of us anyway due to sitting at our desks all day, and it has the added benefit of bringing more energy to your dictation session. I always notice an increase in my speed and total word count when I get a bit of pacing in.

If you would like to pace around your desk, I recommend a 15-30 foot XLR cord and a cushy mat for the area around your desk.

If possible, it's also nice to set up a standing desk. This doesn't have to be complicated—plenty of people just put a box on their regular desk. I have a bookshelf in my living room cleared off and have adjusted the shelf heights for my monitor to be at eye level and my keyboard to be at waist level.

The standing desk is by no means necessary to be comfortable, it's just something I like to have so if I want to adjust something using a keyboard or mouse, I'm set up to comfortably do so.

Finally, I keep a lounge chair right next to my standing desk. When I'm tired of standing, I will totally sit down in the chair and kick my feet up while still dictating. What can I say—my mic and I love to cuddle.

DICTATION ON THE GO

If you take your Dragon on a walk, here are a couple of key reminders that will make your stroll more pleasant and keep you from losing precious words.

Keep your recording sessions short—15-20 minutes always works best for me. This gives me the chance to listen back and check my audio files without being too disruptive to my writing flow.

Do a quick 15 second test and playback before you set out to make sure your equipment is in good working order.

Keep spare parts on hand in case it isn't and you need to trade something out.

Be aware of cords and connections. These can come loose if you are walking around. There's nothing worse than recording a killer writing session only to find out your microphone was unplugged.

Have two separate devices, one for recording and one for carrying your notes. If you only have one device, use it for recording and make a printout of your notes.

Bring spare batteries. Charge your batteries immediately upon returning home.

Use a special bag that is your Walk 'n' Talk bag. Keep all of your equipment in this bag so you don't forget anything the next time you go. I tried a few bags but was most comfortable with a two-strap, lightweight backpack.

Transfer and label your audio files right away when you get home. Use the book, chapter, and scene names and tack on a date at the end. This will help you stay organized.

Additionally, run them through your dictation program right away. You won't know what you accomplished until you complete this step, and getting in this habit will also alert you if there are any problems with your recording setup.

Walking can both wake up your creative energy and also wear you out physically. Find a balance between the two.

Walk in a quiet area and don't skip the wind screen (or clean sock if you prefer). Your mic will pick up the noise around you, and that can affect accuracy when you transcribe.

People may look at you funny while you're out, but you can smugly think to yourself how productive and efficient and awesome you are being. Have they ever written a book? Didn't think so. Game over. You win.

Stay safe on the trail. Keep in mind that you will not only be on a quieter trail, you will also be absorbed in your work and not paying close attention to things going on around you. Also, you'll be carrying quite a bit of expensive equipment. Watch for muggers, especially if you are in a major city.

Lastly, have fun! If writing this way isn't fun for you, what's the point?

PART C: COMMANDS

I hear from authors all the time, "I can't stand doing punctuation while I dictate." Learning dictation commands is one of the biggest hurdles to getting started, so here are some of my best tips to simplify the process:

WATCH THE SCREEN

Once you are up and going with Dragon in your daily life, you won't need to check the screen. But when you're just starting out, you'll need to monitor the screen to make sure your words are appearing properly.

There will be errors, especially at first. Resist the urge to correct these. One thing I do is just repeat the phrase again if it showed up as gobbledygook. It's simple enough to delete the gobbledygook phrase in edits.

Something to watch out for is stray commands. There are several modes in Dragon and the two you must keep an eye on are Dictation mode and Command mode. In dictation mode, your speech gets translated to text on the screen. In command mode, your speech gets translated to a command that causes changes in state on your computer. For example, you can command Dragon to open files, close files, save files, move the cursor around on the screen, and more.

Dragon attempts to switch between these two modes depending on the context it understands. Sometimes this causes problems in your dictation. For example, you could say, "She is a bad girl" and Dragon may mistake the word bad for "bold." It would then do something stupid, like find the phrase "She is a" and apply the Bold style to it.

This issue wouldn't be so bad, but Command mode can get you into major trouble if you aren't paying attention. For example, it could accidentally highlight a large section of text and then dictate over it, which would delete the text. It could also switch programs to something that doesn't allow dictation and you could be speaking into your computer with no input getting recorded.

These issues are solvable if you notice them early, just as they begin to happen.

You can turn Command mode off while you're dictating to help with this problem, but it doesn't fix every single instance of it. The best solution I've found is just to pay attention.

I don't always stare at my screen when I write anymore, especially when I'm pacing, but I do watch at a distance to see that the text is still being inputed into the page. I also write in such small chunks that I have plenty of check-in points where I stop dictating and quickly review the content I've just created. You'll have to find a process that works for you, so keep this in mind as you go.

MINIMIZE YOUR DICTATION COMMANDS

It's easy to get overwhelmed with everything you could learn to do with dictation. My philosophy for a happy relationship is to learn as few commands as possible when you first start.

You can learn hundreds of commands for dictation, but you only need five to get you through 90% of the writing situations you'll face. I recommend learning:

- Period
- Comma
- Open quote
- Close quote
- New line

Yes, there's stuff you can't do using these five commands, but you can correct those few instances in edits to start out with.

As your comfort with dictation grows, you can then add a few other common ones to your skill set:

- Question mark
- Exclamation mark
- Dash (this produces an em dash)
- Hyphen
- Colon
- Semicolon

Once you have these 11 commands down, you'll now be able to get through about 99% of the writing situations you'll face. From there, whenever you find yourself stuck, take a quick pause (tell Dragon to "go to sleep") and use Google to look up how to do it. Learn as you go—it's totally fine!

USE YOUR INTUITION TO LEARN NEW COMMANDS

Another option is to guess. Sounds stupid, but here's the thing—Dragon isn't trying to trick you. Need a parenthesis? You can be pretty sure that "Open Parenthesis" will work.

(And it does.) Need an ellipsis? You can be pretty confident that "Ellipsis" will work. (And it does.)

Pop quiz! Can you guess how to close a parenthesis? (Look it up if you want the answer—but I'm guessing you probably won't need to.)

Your Dragon is like a dog and responds in mostly the way you expect it to when you tell it what to do. (There are a few times when it pees in your slippers—but we'll get to those in a minute.)

LOVE YOUR DRAGON'S QUIRKINESS OTHERWISE

While most punctuation is intuitive, I'll admit that creating bullet points threw me for a loop at first.

The reason is because Dragon doesn't consider bullets punctuation, it considers them formatting.

Punctuation is easily inputted because Dragon treats it as a text character. That's why "Period" is no different than "toaster" to Dragon.

Formatting is treated differently, though in that it must be applied to text that is already written.

Bringing this back to bullets, in order to create a bulleted list you must apply the bullet to a snippet of text. You do this by saying "bullet" after you speak the text. So if you want to make a bulleted list that contains ham, cheese, mustard, and whole-grain bread, you would say "ham bullet cheese bullet mustard bullet whole-grain bread bullet."

(Obviously it's lunch time in my neck of the woods.)

Similarly, other formatting commands like "bold" and "italic" also need to be applied to text. You can say "bold that" and it will apply the "Bold" style to your last block of text.

You will have to do a little memorizing that will come with experience as to what is treated as a text character and what is treated as formatting. It's a little annoying and maybe confusing at first, but you will get the hang of it. Remember, your Dragon just thinks a tad bit differently than you at times.

DELETING, SELECTING, SPELLING

A common convention that your Dragon uses is the idea of applying an action or a format to the last chunk of content you spoke. Mess up? Use the phrase, "Delete that" to back up. It will delete the last phrase you spoke (usually a sentence or half sentence, depending on your cadence).

"Select that" and "Spell that" are also fantastic phrases to use for correcting minor mistakes you make as you go.

JUST KEEP GOING

Although I do use "Delete that" regularly, I also am a huge fan of the strategy of continuing on. A lot of the time when I make a mistake, I just try the phrase again. For example, if I meant to use a comma instead of a period, I just pause and say, "comma." Later while I'm editing, I delete the offending and misplaced period, no harm done.

TAKE THE PATH OF LEAST RESISTANCE

You can make Dragon waaay more complicated than it is.

For example, New Line is easier than Next Line or New Paragraph. Say them out loud and feel the difference. Can you get away with the first one?

Similarly, you can say "Bold that," "Set that bold," or "Format that bold." Can you get away with the first one?

Also, there are times when you can just skip a command. For example, forget about learning Cap, Caps On, Caps

Off. Your Dragon is pretty smart and will capitalize when it makes sense—at the beginning of a sentence, a quote, or when you say a proper name or location. I have never ever said these three commands and actually didn't even know you were supposed to for several years! It's only recently when Write Better, Faster came out and a bunch of authors told me they couldn't stand managing their uppercase and lowercase as they were writing. I was like, [tilts head to the side], "Huh?"

Sometimes over-training yourself can actually make you worse at dictation. I'd rather add a capital letter once in a blue moon than have that on my mind the entire time I'm writing. So look for the easiest way to do something and fix the rest in post. It doesn't need to be perfect, especially since it's a first draft and you will probably edit it a few more times anyway.

PRACTICE AND MEMORIZE FREQUENTLY USED COMMAND COMBINATIONS

You've got the basic building blocks, now let's make some command phrases! Here are a few examples of what I mean:

- New line open quote (to start a new paragraph of dialog)
- Comma close quote he said period (to end a dialog line with a tag)
- Semicolon however comma (to connect two sentences)

These will vary depending on your writing style, but it's important to practice them so they become one fluid phrase. Dragon will not only respond better when you speak them with confidence and clarity (rather than fumbling through or speaking them slowly—that just confuses your

Dragon), they will also become second nature. That means you are back to focusing on your writing rather than the commands, which is always our goal!

MORE DRILLS

I'm generally not a fan of dictation drills which is why I've made it through this entire book without giving you any. However, many of you will want additional training exercises to run through with your Dragon. For that, I recommend Scott Baker's work as he has been working with dication since the 1990's and really knows his stuff.

PART D: FRUSTRATIONS

There are some things Dragon just isn't well-equipped to do. Here are a few of the frustrations I've had, plus the workarounds I've found:

CODIFY PROPER NAMES AND PLACES

If you are writing fiction, you'll probably feel the pain of your Dragon messing up all of your characters' names. Dragon is one of those people who says, "Hi, nice to meet you." [Two seconds later.] "Remind me of your name? I'm so bad with names."

(Sidenote: is anyone really "bad with names"?)

Dragon's inability to remember might hurt your feelings, but there's a simple enough workaround and also a long-term solution.

First, you can train your Dragon to learn someone's name with the command Spell That. It might, however, take a lot of effort and he could continue to mess it up in the future. This might mean that you are spelling your character's name over and over again throughout your manuscript. Multiply that effort times the hundreds of first names, last names, and made up places in your high fantasy and boy are you in for a fun time!

It's debatable whether you can really blame your Dragon for this—after all, he said he was BAD WITH NAMES.

In the meantime, while you are trying to teach him manners and maybe quizzing him with flashcards, you can also take the high road and be polite when he gets it wrong.

I call this strategy "Answering to Toby" (and yes, that's a Friends reference).

It involves making it easy on your Dragon by feeding him with names that he already remembers. These are typically Top 100 Baby Names that he has already been preprogrammed with.

My character Rykken is now "Ryan."

My character Thessa is now "Tessa."

Dragon is happy with "Nicole," but will never ever get "Nikoli" correct.

You can be frustrated by this and make a huge fuss or (worse) give up, or you can play it cool and answer to Toby because, donuts.

I choose the latter strategy and encourage you to do so as well. Why make life hard on yourself? Just use a code name and do a Replace All on your manuscript. Done and done.

MAKE A GRIEVANCE LIST

Along the same lines, keep a list of words and phrases that your Dragon frequently messes up. For example, my Dragon translates "already" to "Artie" on a regular basis. Yes, it's annoying, so write it down and bring it up at your couple's therapy session later this week.

You can use the list you create to train your Dragon later, after your writing session is done. In the shorter term, you can run a Find and Replace All on your manuscript right before you edit. Combining the two approaches will save your marriage, now that the honeymoon period is over.

TRAIN YOUR DRAGON LATER

In general, I'm a huge fan of looking up commands and digging into the owner's manual for your software. There is tons of online support for Dragon and you can find cool PDF cheat sheets online that you can print out and keep by your desk.

But don't overdo it or put off writing in search of the newest phrase you can use to talk to your Dragon. The worst mistake I see writers make with dictation is this idea that they need to finish "training their Dragon" before they start writing their book. This is the procrastination police and I'm calling you out, here and now!

Remember, you don't need to know how to fully use the software to get started using it. When you learned to type, did you ever think, "Wow, I really need to learn the exact placements of every finger in every situation before I write my 5-paragraph 'What I did this Summer' essay?"

I still have no idea whether I should use my right hand or left hand to hit "Y" on the keyboard—and it doesn't matter in the slightest. It hasn't affected my success and my readers haven't got a clue that I am a slightly dysfunctional typist. I've been typing since childhood and I still discover new keys on my keyboard to this day.

Dictation is the exact same way. Yes, it's great to know the easiest, most perfect command for doing something—but a lot of the time the slightly inefficient command works just fine. I don't know any shortcuts on my computer either, but I get by with a few mouse clicks instead, even if it takes a few seconds longer.

Your dictation skills don't need to be perfect, you just need to start. Learn enough to simply get started, and the whole process of adding this skill set will be much easier.

And always remember your ultimate goal: to add words to your manuscript. Prioritize this at all times while learning dictation, and you should be just fine!

Chapter 5
FREQUENTLY ASKED QUESTIONS

For this last chapter, I wanted to share my answers to some of the most frequently asked questions I receive from other authors. Most of these have already been addressed somewhere else in the text, but I always find it useful to reread the same concept multiple ways. Furthermore, in this chapter I'm going to be very explicit about how to solve each issue, just in case you've skimmed past it elsewhere.

If you have a question about dictation, feel free to shoot it to me at contact@monicaleonelle.com—I'm happy to answer it in a future blog post, or maybe even a future edition of this book!

WILL MY ACCENT AFFECT MY ACCURACY?

There are options within Dragon to choose the accent that best matches your own. You can toggle between a variety of supported languages, and if you are dictating in English, you have the option to choose a U.S, U.K, or Australian dialect.

For regional accents, there's no specific support at the time of this book's writing. However, Dragon should be able to handle any English accent due to its profiling capabilities.

So will your accent affect accuracy? Maybe. While I can't confirm, my guess is that in the United States, someone with a midwest accent will have a slightly easier time than someone with a thick southerner accent or someone with a Boston or New York accent. There may be similar situations for other English-speaking countries as well. This may mean that you have a slight handicap in getting started with dictation, but it doesn't mean it can't work for you—just that you may need to spend a little more time training than other authors you know.

My recommendation is whatever your accent, test. Try out the different dialect options until you find the one that works best for you, regardless of whether it matches the dialect you would best fall under. You truly never know what might work!

And remember, there are accuracy problems due to accents and accuracy problems due to getting used to the software. Before you assume it's entirely your accent, be sure to try some of the other tips on accuracy that I've already shared.

WILL MY WRITING STYLE CHANGE?

Yes, it might—but this isn't necessarily a bad thing. The biggest change I found with dictation is that I was forced to draft without editing. This meant that my first draft was often rougher.

That said, my first draft was also usually more free-flowing, and I surprised myself much more often!

Now that I've been using the software for awhile, I would say my writing style while typing is about the same as my writing style while dictating. A lot of this has to do with a concept that has become a theme throughout this book, which is, "get to a place where dictation is just another tool." Because I'm so comfortable with dictation, the input method fades into the background easily for me. The sentences form in my head, and how they get onto the screen is trivial.

I'm a firm believer that to write faster and write well, you must separate your draft from your edits. Again, it might not be a bad thing for your writing style to change—but it's really up to you and you should do what works best.

HOW DO I MAINTAIN WRITING FLOW?

Writing flow comes from many different productivity strategies converging. I spent a whole chapter in Write Better, Faster on the concept of flow and focus, so I won't rehash those strategies here.

There are two main areas where dictation can get in the way of flow, in my experience.

The first one is separating the writing process from the editing process. If you aren't used to working this way, it is going to change your writing style and that will take some adjustment. That said, once you master this concept (using either a keyboard or dictation) you will find yourself in flow much more easily while writing.

The second one is memorizing and using the dictation commands while you write. This, again, is just a matter of practice. Once you get used to dictating, those commands are going to come to you just as easily as your fingers move across your keyboard. The tool is going to fade into the background, and all you'll be left with are your words.

Again, it all comes down to practice—and the best way to practice in my opinion is somewhere other than your book manuscript. Email, text, or web content is a fantastic place to start.

If you are wondering how long this frustration might be a part of your life, I would say give yourself ten full hours of serious dictation (dictation where you're truly trying to be productive and not just playing around with it) to see if your writing style adjusts and/or the commands start to feel like second nature.

If it's still an issue after that, come back to this book and give it a reread (it's short, so this should only take 90 minutes or so) to see if you've missed something or if some advice makes more sense now that you've done the training work. Also, feel free to reach out to me at contact@monicaleonelle.com—I'll do whatever I can to help!

DO YOU USE DICTATION FOR REVISION?

I don't. I don't believe that any writer should use dictation for revision unless they are either very good at dictation commands or are forced to due to a health condition. Revision is difficult due to cursor placement and options for selection and deletion.

The only sort of revision I might do using dictation is while I'm writing the draft. I typically revise as I go only when I make a mistake using the command, "Delete That." This deletes the last "phrase" you've spoken into your software. This sort of on-the-spot revision is helpful when you make a mistake that's easy enough to correct right away.

I do all other revisions with a keyboard, which I recommend for you as well. Before I do a content revision, I typically do a Replace All or cleanup revision where I go through and fix any major repeated mistakes (primarily characters names and other frustrations that we discussed in the last chapter).

I also sometimes do this as I go. For example, if I'm reading along and see a name that is frequently misspelled two paragraphs in, I do a quick Find + Replace All on it. Easy!

One thing I want to add is that dictation can actually help you make fewer mistakes, particularly with misspelled words and homophones (a subset of homonyms with same sound, different spelling and meaning, e.g. theirs, there's). It all depends on how you already write.

WHAT IS THE BEST WAY TO TRAIN MY DRAGON?

Training your Dragon over time is primarily using it… which… sucks if you hate using it due to poor results.

We've talked about tips and strategies to train your Dragon throughout this book already, but I wanted to give one last pep talk if you are still struggling with the concept of training your Dragon.

My best response to this question, aside from providing the same strategies I've already shared in this book, is this:

DON'T MAKE TRAINING YOUR DRAGON A HUGE PRODUCTION!

Here's why: the software is 98-99% accurate for most people out of the box. It's pretty hard to train it to 100%, and in my opinion, that kind of effort is likely in the 20 of the 80/20 Pareto principle.

I also believe (crossed fingers) that in a few years the software will get there on its own. It's very close. Thus, we'll be able to use it the same exact way we do today and we'll see the accuracy improve, without any additional effort on our parts. Win!

So, if you want to gain the benefits of Dragon, you do have to first accept that Dragon isn't going to give you perfect output.

This is why I recommend using it on lower stakes tasks in your writing process. I use it primarily on notes and first drafts, where 100% accuracy isn't needed. This is truly no different than the results you'd get from a keyboard. No seasoned writer would ever tell a new writer to correct every keyboard mistake as he goes on his first draft... this is basically the same advice, just with a different input.

Additionally, I would never edit a manuscript with Dragon—it's possible, but unless you are forced to because you have no hands or arms, it's not worth it, at least at this time. Instead, these are the few strategies I use when I make a mistake:

LEAVE IT AND FIX IT IN THE FIRST ROUND OF EDITS

If it's something that messes up often, make a note of it and Replace All before I start editing. Train this particular word later using their vocabulary editor

Say "Delete That" which affects the last "phrase" you spoke into the software. Once the phrase is gone, try again

If the mistake is not easy to delete, pause and start fresh with what I wanted to say. Leave the extraneous content for the first round of edits. This is essentially the "keep going" principle you would use with a first draft anyway, regardless of the input device

It takes me maybe a few minutes to correct a piece of non-fiction text using these strategies for mistakes. This section of the book would take me an extra two minutes or so to correct. Fiction is a bit longer, of course, but I also notice that I rewrite more stuff anyway and the errors don't bother me as much.

The bottom line: Unless your accuracy is truly lower than about 95% with no user errors (all of the errors are on Dragon's part), don't stress about training your Dragon that last 5%. It's like training yourself on keyboard. Doesn't really matter if you're perfect or a pecker, as long as you get the words out.

Lastly, don't forget the reason behind training your Dragon, which is to get your ideas onto the screen faster than you could with a keyboard. I truly believe that when writers focus on the work, it makes it so much easier and more satisfying to work with dictation.

Good luck!

ADDITIONAL RESOURCES

ORIGINAL ARTICLES

You can find my weekly articles at

ProseOnFire.com/blog/

Don't forget to sign up for more information on future books in this series:

ProseOnFire.com/Storytellers/

So many good books coming up!

TRACKING AND BOOKS

Want to test whether dictation really does help you write faster? Get my tracking spreadsheet completely free!

ProseOnFire.com/tracking

Write Better, Faster: How To Triple Your Writing Speed and Write More Every Day is about how I reached speeds of 4000+ words per hour! I also share my 2-month experiment in establishing a consistent writing habit. If you want the full behind-the-scenes tour of optimizing your writing speed, this is the book that has it.

ProseOnFire.com/WriteFaster/

The 8-Minute Writing Habit: Create a Consistent Writing Habit That Works With Your Busy Lifestyle is for busy people who don't have time for tons of experimentation and tracking. They just want to write more words per week, per month, without having to overhaul their lifestyles. Perfect for busy professionals, students, and moms and dads!

ProseOnFire.com/8Minutes/

5000 Words Per Hour by Chris Fox is a pretty cool book on writing faster that's similar to mine... plus he has an app that helps you track your word counts!

MORE FROM MONICA

Looking to build an email list? Check out the easy-to-implement "3-step Email List-Building Framework" (webinar replay): ProseOnFire.com/3step

Trying to write a fiction book or books? You will probably love my "First 5 Pages Scorecard," which helps you rate how effective your novel opening chapter is in hooking your readers. Perfect if you are trying to optimize your ebook sample! ProseOnFire.com/first1000

Want to get a list of EVERY tool I use for my business (including my full dictation setup, all the software I use, and more?) Get my "Author Equipment List" so you never need to search for the perfect tool again.

ProseOnFire.com/equipment

REMEMBER!

If you enjoyed this book, there are two things you can do that will really help spread the word about it:

#1: YOU CAN WRITE A REVIEW

As an independent author, reviews are one of the most important ways I have to get the word out. Your review will encourage others to grab the book. You can share anything, but here are a few ideas:

- What you liked about the book
- What you didn't like about the book
- Your favorite chapter/part in the book
- Three things you are going to implement from the book
- The results you hope to get or have already gotten from the book

Go to ProseOnFire.com/pofd if you want to leave a review and help others discover a new way to write!

Also, make sure you send it to me at monicaleonelle@ gmail.com (my personal email address) so I can thank you properly for your support.

When you do, also tell me a little about yourself (optional, of course). Perhaps name ONE thing you want to change about your writing process. I'd love to hear from you—my email pals often inspire blog posts, which I love to dedicate to them!

#2: YOU CAN TELL THREE AUTHORS YOU KNOW ABOUT THIS BOOK

There are probably a few author friends who could benefit from this information, right? Why not send them an email or text with the title of the book right now? Takes just a few seconds, and you can do it from your phone!

Email or Text: Check out Dictate Your Book by Monica Leonelle on Amazon! I enjoyed it and thought you would too.

I greatly appreciate all your support! Please let me know if I'm able to help you with anything in the future: monicaleonelle@gmail.com.

SIGN UP FOR MORE

Be the first to know about upcoming books.

ProseOnFire.com/Storytellers/

ABOUT THE AUTHOR

Monica Leonelle was born in Germany and spent her childhood jet-setting around the world with her American parents. Her travels include most of the United States and Europe, as well as Guam, Japan, South Korea, Australia, and the Philippines.

She started publishing independently in 2009 and has since published over half a million words of fiction spread across five series, Socialpunk, Waters Dark and Deep, Emma + Elsie, and two under a pen name. In 2014, she published 8 books and one short story.

She writes about indie publishing at ProseOnFire.com. Her most recent non-fiction book, Write Better, Faster, has earned raving reviews from the independent publishing community for going deeper than anyone else into the topic of writing speed. She currently averages around 3,000 words per hour and writes 25,000+ words per week (most weeks).

Before becoming an independent author, Monica led digital marketing efforts at Inc. 100 companies like Hansen's Natural and Braintree.

Monica is a lifetime member of Sigma Pi Sigma honor fraternity and was a 2007 Chicago Business Fellow, graduating with an MBA from the Chicago Booth School of Business at 25 years old. She holds a Bachelor of Science in Computer Science with a minor in Physics from Truman State University.

She's been an avid blogger of marketing and business trends since 2007. Her ideas have been featured in AdAge, The Huffington Post, the AMEX OpenForum, GigaOm, Mashable, Social Media Today, and the Christian Science Monitor. In 2009, she was named one of the top 25 Tweeters in the city of Chicago by ChicagoNow, a subsidiary of the Chicago Tribune.

COPYRIGHT

Library of Congress Cataloging-in-Publication Data is available.

Spaulding House Publishing

600 S. Dearborn

Chicago, IL 60605

First Edition

First Printing

Author: Monica Leonelle

Printed in Great Britain
by Amazon